HAITI

By Jagger Youssef and Joanne Mattern

EXPLORING WORLD CULTURES

Cavendish Square

Published in 2027 by Cavendish Square Publishing, LLC
2544 Clinton Street, Buffalo, NY 14224

Second Edition

Website: cavendishsq.com

Library of Congress Cataloging-in-Publication Data

Names: Youssef, Jagger author | Mattern, Joanne, 1963- author
Title: Haiti / Jagger Youssef and Joanne Mattern.
Description: New York : Cavendish Square Publishing, [2027] | Series: Exploring World Cultures | Includes index.
Identifiers: LCCN 2026004693 (print) | LCCN 2026004694 (ebook) | ISBN 9781502677082 library binding | ISBN 9781502677075 paperback | ISBN 9781502677099 ebook
Subjects: LCSH: Haiti
Classification: LCC F1915.2 .Y68 2027 (print) | LCC F1915.2 (ebook) | DDC 972.94--dc23/eng/20260218
LC record available at https://lccn.loc.gov/2026004693
LC ebook record available at https://lccn.loc.gov/2026004694

Writers: Jagger Youssef; Joanne Mattern (second edition)
Editor: Therese Shea
Designer: Deanna Lepovich

The photographs in this book are used by permission and through the courtesy of: Cover, p. 13 glenda/Shutterstock.com; p. 4 Emilie Rusch/Alamy Photos; p. 5 AustralianCamera/Shutterstock.com; p. 6 olenadesign/Shutterstock.com; p. 7 Wirestock Creators/Shutterstock.com; p. 8 PJF Military Collection/Alamy Photos; p. 9 Toussaint Louverture - Girardin/Wikimedia Commons; p. 10 zmotions/Shutterstock.com; p. 11 NurPhoto SRL/Almay Photos; p. 12 Janusz Pienkowski/Shutterstock.com; p. 14 Aleksandr Rybalko/Shutterstock.com; p. 15 Haiti deforestation/Wikimedia Commons; p. 16 christian kober/Alamy Photos; p. 17 naTsumi/Shutterstock.com; p. 18 Sylvie Corriveau/Shutterstock.com; p. 19 Agencja FotograEczna Caro/Alamy Photos; p. 20 Haiti Saut-d'Eau/Wikimedia Commons; p. 21 ilpo musto/Alamy Photos; p. 22 EWY Media/Shutterstock.com; p. 23, 26 arindambanerjee/Shutterstock.com; p. 25 (top) blickwinkel/Alamy Photos; p. 25 (bottom) Sergii Koval/Shutterstock.com; p. 27 Ursula Page/Shutterstock.com; p. 28 Grazyna Bonati/Almay Photos; p. 29 Matthew Yoder/Shutterstock.com.

CPSIA compliance information: Batch #CS27CSQ: For further information contact Cavendish Square Publishing LLC at 1-877-980-4450.

Printed in United States of America

CONTENTS

INTRODUCTION

Haiti is a small nation in the Caribbean Sea. It's the western part of an island shared with the Dominican Republic. Haiti is a land of great natural beauty. It's quite mountainous, but has plains and beaches too.

Though Haiti isn't large, it's densely populated. This means many people live closely together. More than 11 million people lived in Haiti in 2024. Most live in cities. Others live and work on farms.

The people of Haiti are called Haitians.

Long ago, Haiti was a **colony** of Spain and then France. **Enslaved** Africans were forced to work for Europeans. After a group overthrew the government, Haiti became an independent, or free, nation in 1804. But the nation and its people went through years of problems, which have lasted through present day.

Much of the nation is poor. Still, they have a culture, or way of life, that is much like the outside world. They enjoy family, food, games, and holidays. Let's learn about Haiti and its people.

On this map, you can see that Haiti is southeast of the United States.

GEOGRAPHY

The island shared by Haiti and the Dominican Republic has a name: Hispaniola. The Atlantic Ocean lies to the north of the island. The island of Tortuga lies just off Haiti's northern coast. The Gulf of Gonâve lies to the west. Gonâve Island, part of Haiti, is located here. Two **peninsulas** stick out into the sea around the Gulf of Gonâve. To the south is the Caribbean Sea.

FACT!

Haiti's highest peak is Pic la Selle in the southeast. It is 8,793 feet (2,680 m) above sea level.

Haiti makes up about one-third of the island of Hispaniola.

In all, Haiti covers 10,714 square miles (27,750 square kilometers). It is about 55 miles (89 kilometers) southeast of Cuba. A narrow strip of water called the Windward Passage lies between the two countries.

Haiti has a tropical climate. This means the island is often hot and wet, though some parts are very dry. **Hurricanes** commonly come ashore.

The small country of Haiti has five mountain ranges.

A NAME FROM HISTORY

The country's name is from the word *hayti*, which means "land of the mountains" in the **Indigenous** Taíno language.

HISTORY

When Christopher Columbus arrived on Hispaniola in 1492, the Taíno people had been there for hundreds of years. Columbus claimed the island for Spain and enslaved the Taíno.

In 1697, Spain gave the western part of the island to France. France called its colony Saint-Domingue. Hundreds of thousands of Africans were sent to Haiti as enslaved workers. They grew sugarcane and coffee.

After the Haitian Revolution, thousands of formerly enslaved people helped build this large fortress called La Citadelle in Haiti. It was meant to guard Haiti from European forces.

General Toussaint Louverture is considered one of the founding fathers of Haiti. He died in a French prison in 1803.

FACT!

Spain once controlled the whole island on which Haiti is found. The Spanish named the island Hispaniola ("Little Spain").

In 1791, Toussaint Louverture, who had been enslaved, led a **rebellion** against France. Haiti became independent in 1804. Jean-Jacques Dessalines became the first ruler. He was killed in 1806. Many years of fighting for control followed.

The Duvalier family ruled Haiti as **dictators** from 1957 to 1986. In 1990, Jean-Bertrand Aristide was elected president. He was forced from office two times. Following years of government troubles, President Jovenel Moïse was killed in 2021. Haiti hasn't had a permanent, or lasting, president since that year.

LED BY COUNCIL

In 2024, Haiti's leaders formed a group called the presidential council. Its job is to bring **democracy** back to Haiti.

GOVERNMENT

Haiti is called a semi-presidential **republic**. That means the president shares power with a prime minister. The government has three parts. These are the executive, legislative, and judicial branches. Haiti's president is elected by the Haitian people to a five-year term. They cannot serve more than two terms. The president represents the nation and is called the head of state. They choose the prime minister, who acts as head of government.

The Haitian flag has the saying, **L'union fait la force**, *meaning "Unity makes strength."*

Leaders hope to have an election in 2026 for all government positions.

FACT!

Haiti's constitution, its highest set of laws, was approved by the people in 1987.

The legislative branch is called the National Assembly. It's divided into the Senate and the Chamber of Deputies. Members of the National Assembly make the laws.

The judicial branch runs Haiti's courts. The highest court is the Court of Cassation.

Haiti hasn't had an election since 1996. That means its government hasn't worked according to its constitution for many years.

TROUBLED TIMES

As of early 2026, gangs controlled most of Haiti's capital city of Port-au-Prince.

THE ECONOMY

About half of all Haitians work on farms. They grow rice, corn, yams, mangoes, bananas, and sugarcane. Farmers also raise chickens, goats, and cattle. Most farmers only grow enough food to feed their families. Some also sell food in markets. Many women bring food and goods from the countryside to sell in the city. They're called the Madan Sara.

Five gourdes is called the Haitian dollar. People sometimes use U.S. dollars too.

MONEY

Haitian money is called the gourde (or goud). In 2026, one gourde was worth less than 1 cent in U.S. money.

More Haitians are moving to cities for work. Those with factory jobs make clothes, cement, and other products. Some factories are owned by U.S. companies. The United States is the country that does the most trade with Haiti.

People from other countries used to visit Haiti. This brought money into the country. However, government problems and gangs have stopped visitors for now.

FACT!

Haiti is the poorest country in the Caribbean. More than half of all Haitians live in poverty.

Haitian women carry bananas to a market.

THE ENVIRONMENT

Haiti's nickname was once the Pearl of the Antilles (Islands) because of its great beauty and rich **natural resources**. The Massif du Nord mountain range stretches across Haiti's northern peninsula. The Noires Mountains are located in the middle of the country. The Massif de la Selle mountain range is in the south. Between these mountain ranges are flat plains. Many farms are located here.

In the waters around Haiti are fish, dolphins, and pilot whales. Crabs, mollusks, and sponges live in coral reefs. On land, frogs and iguanas love the warm, wet weather. Turtles, snakes, and bats live here too.

Haiti has 250 different kinds of birds such as the Dominican tody, shown here.

Deforestation is a problem in Haiti. This is the act of cutting down trees for farming, building, or firewood. People need wood for fuel so it's a hard problem to fix.

FACT!

Deforestation takes homes from animals and leads to problems such as landslides and flooding.

A photo of the border from high above shows deforested Haiti next to the Dominican Republic.

RIVER PROBLEMS

Haiti's longest river is the Artibonite. Deforestation and trash have spoiled its waters. It has few fish today.

THE PEOPLE TODAY

Most Haitians have African roots. Their **ancestors** were enslaved and forced to work for Europeans. Some people have ancestors from both Africa and Europe. A small number of Haitians have Indigenous Taíno ancestors.

The National Palace, where the president lives, was damaged in a 2010 earthquake. It still hasn't been rebuilt.

NATURAL DISASTERS

Haitians have had to deal with dangerous natural events including hurricanes and **earthquakes**. Earthquakes in 2010 and 2021 killed thousands of people and destroyed many buildings. Rebuilding has been very slow.

Haitians with ancestors from Europe have controlled most of the nation's wealth and power, but they're a small part of the population. On the other hand, most Black Haitians are very poor. This has caused problems between these two groups.

The country's broken government, gang problems, and crime have made life hard for many Haitians. Some have chosen to move to other countries, including the Dominican Republic and the United States.

FACT!

About 1 million Haitians live in the United States as of 2024.

In cities, Haitians get around on small colorful buses or trucks called tap-taps.

LIFESTYLE

All of Haiti's cities are crowded. Some homes are poorly made with concrete bricks. Those with more wealth have nicer homes.

In the countryside, the houses are built with wood or clay. The roofs are made of palm leaves or sheets of tin. These houses often have mud floors and no electricity or running water. Country homes usually have one or two rooms.

Housing in some areas of Port-au-Prince looks like this.

Most schools in Haiti are run by religious groups or aid groups from other countries.

FACT!
About 3 million of Haiti's 11 million people live in Port-au-Prince, Haiti's largest city.

Haitian children are supposed to go to school from ages six to fifteen. However, many families cannot afford fees that come with going to school. Few children finish school. Rich families may send their children to schools in other countries. Violence in the country has also made it hard for children to go to school regularly.

GETTING AROUND

Most roads in Haiti are dirt. Most people don't own a car, so walking or taking a bus is often the way to get around.

RELIGION

Religion is a key part of life for many Haitians. Most Haitians are Christians, or followers of Jesus Christ. Many are a kind of Christian called Roman Catholic. The Spanish brought this religion to Haiti. The French also practiced Catholicism. Enslaved workers were forced to accept the religion. Some people in Haiti today are different kinds of Protestant Christians.

Every July, Haitians travel to the Saut d'Eau waterfalls to bathe there. This site is very special for those who practice Catholicism and Vodou.

RELIGIONS' ROLES

Different religious groups spread their faith while bringing aid, health care, and education to Haitians.

Prayer, song, drumming, and dance are part of the practice of Vodou.

FACT!
About half of all Haitians are Roman Catholic. About one-fourth are Protestant.

Many Haitians practice a religion called Vodou, or Voodoo. These beliefs combine parts of West African religions and Roman Catholicism. Enslaved Africans brought Vodou to Haiti in the 1500s and 1600s. Those who practice Vodou honor spirits as well as God. They also believe Vodou can heal. It was named one of Haiti's official religions in 2003. Haitians often practice Voudou in addition to another religion.

LANGUAGE

Haiti has two official languages: French and Haitian Creole. French is the language used in government and business. However, most Haitians don't speak French. They speak Haitian Creole (KREE-ole). This language mixes French and African words. Haitian Creole also includes some Spanish, English, and Taíno words. In 1987, the new constitution declared Creole an official language alongside French. Many schools still teach classes in French. It's spoken by people with more money too.

FACT!

The Haitian Creole word for this language is Kreyòl.

This sign includes Haitian Creole and English.

People in Haiti's neighbor, the Dominican Republic, speak Spanish. Some Haitians who live along the border also speak some Spanish. Many businesspeople and government leaders may use English too.

Even though nearly all Haitians speak Creole as their first language, most schools teach in French.

CREOLES

Haitian Creole is just one kind of creole. Creole languages mix other languages until they become a lasting language of their own. There are other kinds of French Creole languages spoken on different Caribbean islands.

ARTS AND FESTIVALS

Life can be hard in Haiti, but Haitian arts and festivals are cause for celebration. The biggest holiday in Haiti is Carnival. Carnival is celebrated with street parties and parades. People dance, play music, and wear colorful costumes.

January 1 is Haiti's Independence Day. Haitians celebrate by eating a special soup called *joumou*. It's made of squash, potatoes, and meat. April 7 is when Haitians remember General Toussaint Louverture, and October 17 celebrates the former ruler Jean-Jacques Dessalines. Haitians celebrate many Christian holidays too, including Easter, All Saints' Day, and Christmas.

The arts are also important to Haitians. Haitian paintings and **sculptures** often mix African and European styles. Haiti has a special kind of music called rara. It's lively and uses drums, horns, bells, and sometimes chanting.

Carnival is a season in Haiti. It lasts from January through February or March.

FACT!

Perhaps the most well-known song in Haiti is called Haïti Chérie (Dear Haiti). It's about having pride in the country.

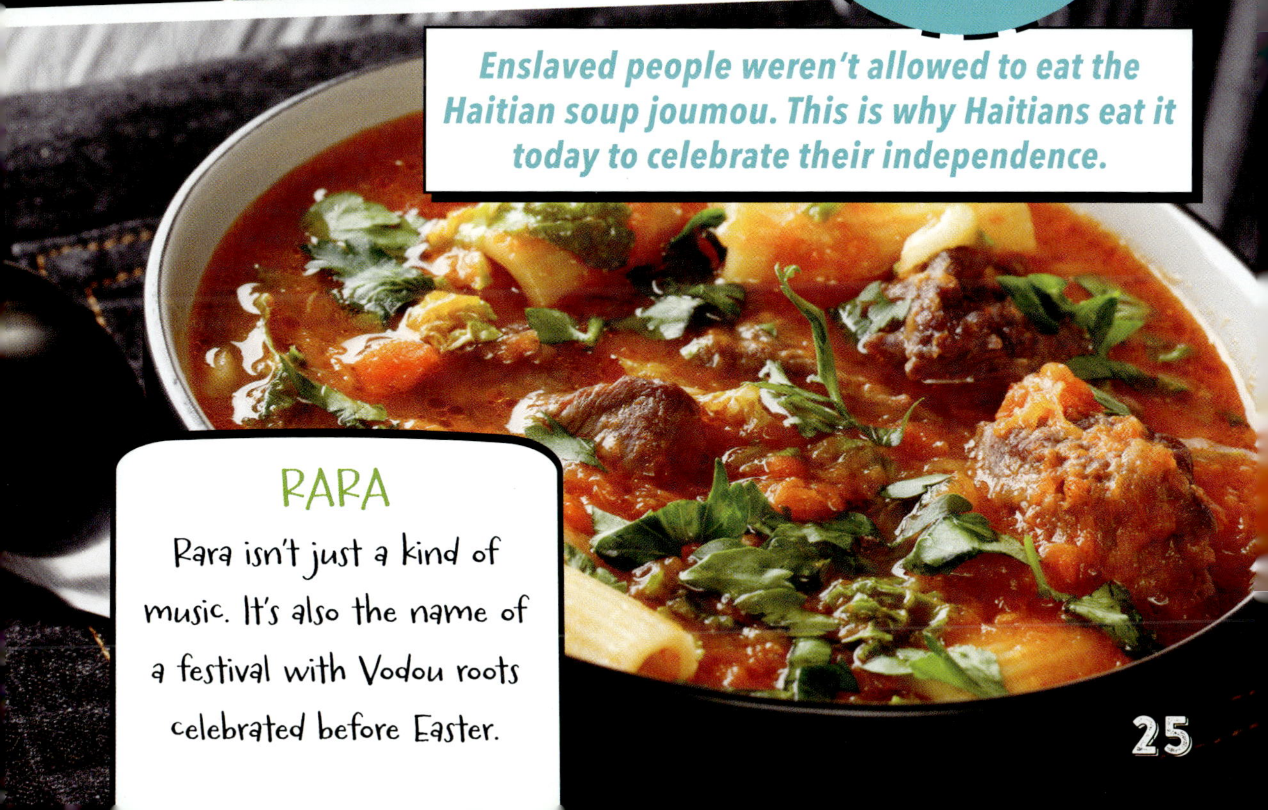

Enslaved people weren't allowed to eat the Haitian soup joumou. This is why Haitians eat it today to celebrate their independence.

RARA

Rara isn't just a kind of music. It's also the name of a festival with Vodou roots celebrated before Easter.

FUN AND PLAY

Soccer is the most popular sport in Haiti. It's called football there. People play soccer wherever they can. For example, in cities, they sometimes block off streets to play. Many schools have soccer teams for boys. Haiti also has a pro soccer league with teams all over the country.

Basketball is also a top sport, especially for young people. Haitians enjoy swimming in the Caribbean Sea and in the country's rivers. Along the coast, people like fishing, sailing, diving, and more.

Young Haitians play soccer in Port-au-Prince.

Games are also popular. Many Haitians play cards and dominoes. They play at home or in the streets.

In Vodou, dancing and drumming are important social activities. People come together to sing and dance.

FACT!

Storytelling is an important custom in Haiti. It's a way to pass on values and ways of life.

Haitians often play dominoes around a table outdoors.

TRADITIONAL GAMES

Other Haitian games include Oslè, a game using goat bones, and Warri, a game in which players move seeds. Both of these use things that people would have and not need to buy.

FOOD

Haitian foods mix the cultures that have lived in the country: mostly Taíno, African, Spanish, and French. Dishes often have a lot of flavor, and many are spicy.

Many Haitian meals include rice with beans. Many people would say the national dish is *diri kole ak pwa*, which is rice with beans covered with a sauce and topped with red snapper fish, tomatoes, and onions.

Haiti's tropical climate makes fruits—and fruit juices—easy to find.

COOL DRINKS FOR HOT WEATHER

In Haiti, fresco is made by pouring syrup from tropical fruits over ice. Jus papaye mixes papaya juice, milk, sugar, and ice.

Common vegetables are potatoes, yam, okra, and cabbage. Common fruits are avocados, pineapples, and mangoes. Fried plantains are a snack.

Not all meals are eaten with meat since meat is costly. However, goat, chicken, pork, and beef may be added to some dishes. Near the coast, people eat fish, crab, and other seafood. Many cities around the world have Haitian restaurants where people can get a taste of this rich culture.

FACT!

Manger-Yam (Eat Yam) Day happens around November 25. It marks the yam harvest.

Another popular and well-known Haitian dish is griyo, or fried pork.

GLOSSARY

ancestor: A relative who lived long before you.

colony: An area under the control of another country.

democracy: The free and equal right of every person to participate in a government.

dictator: One who rules a nation by force.

earthquake: A shaking of the ground caused by the movement of Earth's crust.

enslaved: Having to do with being owned by another person and forced to work without pay under terrible conditions.

hurricane: A powerful storm that forms over water and causes heavy rainfall and high winds.

Indigenous: Having to do with the original or first people in a place.

natural resource: Something in nature that can be used by people.

peninsula: Land area surrounded by water on three sides.

rebellion: A fight to overthrow a government.

republic: A form of government in which the people elect representatives who run the government.

sculpture: A shape created by an artist from stone, wood, metal, or other matter.

FIND OUT MORE

Books

Sommer, Nathan. *The Haiti Earthquake*. Minneapolis, MN: Bellwether Media, 2022.

Vonder Brink, Tracy. *Haiti*. St. Catharines, Ontario: Crabtree Publishing, 2025.

Websites

Haiti
kids.britannica.com/kids/article/Haiti/345703
Britannica Kids provides a review of facts about this country.

Haiti
kids.nationalgeographic.com/geography/countries/article/haiti
National Geographic Kids has more info about Haiti.

Video

Mr. History: A Super Quick History of Haiti
www.youtube.com/watch?v=S-XZLYGILBA
This website has a 5-minute video of Haitian history.

Publisher's note to educators and parents: Our editors have carefully reviewed these websites to ensure that they are suitable for students. Many websites change frequently, however, and we cannot guarantee that a site's future contents will continue to meet our high standards of quality and educational value. Be advised that students should be closely supervised whenever they access the internet.

INDEX